A souvenir guide

Emmetts Garden

Kent

2

The Garden

8

10 A plantsman's paradise
11 The nurseries of James Veitch
12 The age of plant collecting
14 The quest for the dove tree

The Boise Years   18

A Head Gardener's Tale   20

A Children's Garden   22

Tour of the Garden   24
24 The Rose Garden
25 The Alpine and Rock Garden
26 The South Garden
28 The Woodland and Bluebell Bank

Explore the Estate   30

What next for Emmetts?   32

National Trust

A Tale of Two Gardens

Commanding some of the most impressive views over the Weald of Kent, Emmetts Garden stands testament to some of the finest traditions of English garden design of the last 150 years. From its humble Victorian beginnings through to the heyday of twentieth-century high society, it represents a living tribute to the passions, whims and ideals of its former owners. As a much-loved family home the gardens have provided an inspirational backdrop as a place for horticulture and as a space for family relaxation and enjoyment, a tradition which continues to symbolise the spirit of Emmetts today.

During the latter half of the nineteenth century Emmetts evolved from a farmstead to become a desirable Victorian residence, attracting a steady succession of owners. Frederick Lubbock's purchase of the property in 1890 heralded a period of dramatic transformation

Above The wedding cake tree (*Cornus controvosa*)

Opposite The South Garden in autumn

and expansion of the modest Victorian villa garden. He carefully laid out a series of planting areas to indulge his love of horticulture and provide a peaceful setting for his home and family. Closest to the house, he designed a charming suite of ornamental gardens filled with herbaceous plants, bulbs, roses and shrubs. To the south, perched above the wooded glades and dells of the greensand hills, he set aside an area to nurture his growing collection of exotic trees and shrubs.

On Frederick's death in 1927 Charles Watson Boise, an American geologist, became the new owner of the house and gardens. Charles and his wife respected much of the work carried out by Lubbock but also made their own unique impression upon the gardens in other ways. Charles Boise bequeathed Emmetts to the National Trust in 1964, thereby ensuring that the character of these treasured gardens could be preserved for future generations.

Charting the history

Long before Emmetts existed as a distinct place, the high ridge of hills upon which the house now stands formed part of the uncultivated land of the manor and parish of Brasted. This high ground, traditionally known as the 'Chart' (from the Saxon word, *cert* or 'rough common'), served the lower-lying settlements as a place for grazing cattle and pigs. The Domesday Book of 1086 records the Manor of Brasted as having 'wood for pannage of 20 hogs'. Villagers also had commoners' rights to gather peat and underwood for fire fuel, bracken for animal bedding and chertstone for road and building materials.

Earliest evidence of Emmetts appears on eighteenth-century maps when Amets Farm is shown, a site which possibly originated from piece-meal clearance of the wooded common in medieval times. Later inclosure of the commons in the 1850s witnessed further division of land into private ownership, and many of the boundaries, fields and enclosures we are now familiar with came into being.

'Amets' or 'Emmetts' derives from the Old English word for ants and may have referred to the abundance of ant colonies that are found on the sandy soils of the Chart in this locality.

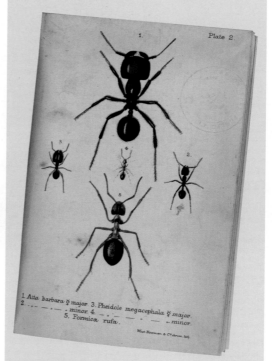

Ilustrations of ants from Sir John Lubbock's book *Ants, Bees, and Wasps. A Record of Observations on the Habits of the Social Hymenoptera*

Left The house, 1890, lithograph

From farm to villa

The earliest known occupier of the farmstead was Edward Smith Biggs who lived here in the mid-eighteenth century. Towards the end of this century the property passed into the ownership of John Malyn (1761–1832), a man of some standing, serving on the Grand Jury at Maidstone Quarter Sessions Court and inheriting a small fortune from his father's estate. He appears to have let the house for some time to a J.L. Minet, a banker who later bought the house and rebuilt it. John lost much of his fortune, reputedly as a result of a loan to Queen Victoria's father that was never repaid. By the 1820s the house had passed to The Rev. John Cleaver Banks (c.1765–1845), a scholar, antiquarian and collector of historical manuscripts.

In 1848 Emmetts Farm was advertised for sale in *The Times* and bought by Sir Samuel Hancock, a cattle dealer and sheep salesman. He built the present house around 1860 on the site of the former farmstead. Little is known of the early layout of the garden under his ownership but mid-nineteenth-century maps reveal tantalising clues to the north and east of the house such as entrance drives, a number of paths linking the east lawn, and an open area with scattered specimen conifers. In 1882 the house passed into the hands of Richard Gibbs after Hancock went bankrupt.

Gibbs' occupancy was relatively short-lived and in 1890 the house and gardens were advertised for sale by Debenham, Tewson, Farmer & Bridgewater. The sale particulars include three lithographs which show evidence of how the gardens looked at this time. Mention is also made of a tennis court forming the centrepiece of the Victorian garden.

Left Frederick Lubbock and his wife Catherine with their children, c.1894

A distinguished family

Frederick Lubbock

The arrival of Frederick Lubbock in 1890 marked the start of a new and exciting chapter in Emmett's history and heralded a period of great change in the layout and design of the garden.

Frederick had grown up at his family home at High Elms near Orpington. Born in 1844 and one of 11 siblings, Frederick's early interests lay in archaeology. He became a member of the Ethnological Society of London. In 1869 he married Catherine Gurney, an heiress of a rich banking family. The Gurneys were Quakers and for many generations had resided at Earlham Hall in Norfolk.

At first Frederick and Catherine took up residence at a house named The Rookery in Downe Village, a stone's throw from High Elms. Within a few years the needs of their young and growing family demanded more space and the couple began to seek a new comfortable home within easy reach of the City of London. Suitably positioned and providing opportunities for renovation and expansion, Emmetts offered the ideal spot. The first improvement was the addition of a third storey to the house, a remarkable project which involved raising the roof on jacks while the floor was added; Frederick used the local building firm Durtnells to undertake the work, a company which is still in existence and is one of the oldest in the country. Their historic association with the property has been happily renewed in more recent times through their

much-appreciated contribution to the Rose Garden; the company were asked to build and supply some hand-crafted garden furniture.

Frederick Lubbock descended from a long-established and distinguished Norfolk family. His father, Sir John William Lubbock, was chairman of the family-founded Lubbock Bank and had lived at High Elms. Here Sir John had enjoyed a good friendship with his neighbour Charles Darwin.

Above John Lubbock (Taken from *A Modern Portrait Gallery* vol. 111 [1881])

Below The Lubbock family at tea, *c*.1910

Left A scene from *A Room with a View* filmed at Emmetts, 1985

Below Frederick and Catherine Lubbock by Roland Pym, 2004

Lord of the flies

Frederick's brother, another Sir John, was a man of many talents. Later to become Lord Avebury he was a Liberal politician and a pioneering naturalist who had an interest in ancient history. Amongst his many works he wrote papers on *Ants Bees and Wasps: A Record of Observations on the Habits of the Social Hymenoptera* (1892) and on *Pre-historic Times, as Illustrated by Ancient Remains and the Manners and Customs of Modern Savages* (1858).

Of his greatest claims to fame are his promotion of the bill that gave us Bank Holidays and early closing. His tireless work in protecting archaeological sites helped pave the way for the introduction of the Ancient Monuments Act of 1882. Never far from his beloved insects he kept a number of ant colonies in miniature greenhouses in his study at High Elms and even took a tame wasp by train to the Pyrenees. It is also claimed that he learned German through practising every morning whilst shaving.

High fliers

Frederick's other ten siblings included Henry, a high sheriff of London, Edgar, a director of the Bank of England and Sir Neville, chairman of the West India Committee. Later generations included Sam Gurney Lubbock, an Eton master renowned for his politeness and patience. Anecdotes tell of an occasion when some of his fellow Etonians hired a barrel organ to play constantly under his window in an attempt to make him angry.

The Garden Creation

Frederick's lasting legacy was his transformation and expansion of the Victorian garden. Strongly influenced by garden designers William Robinson and Gertrude Jekyll, his vision inspired an impressive series of projects that included the addition of an Italianate rose garden and the creation of a rock garden. His final phase of work to the south of the lane has become one of the most treasured parts of the garden for it was here that he indulged in his beloved hobby of plant collecting.

Below Path through spring displays of azaleas

William Robinson and the 'wild garden'

One of Fredrick's greatest influences was gardener and writer William Robinson (1838–1935). Robinson championed the idea of natural, 'wild gardening' and disapproved of the fashion for contrived, formal plantings typical of the Victorian era. Frederick shared this vision and strove to develop a more informal planting style in his work at Emmetts, a characteristic which continues to remain a hallmark of the gardens today.

Born in Ireland, William Robinson became one of the most influential and respected gardeners of his time. A follower of the Victorian Arts and Craft Movement, he advocated the use of hardy perennials, shrubs and climbers to achieve a more natural planting style. These ideas were brought to popularity in his book *The Wild Garden* (1870). This revolutionary approach was a reaction against the formalised and artificial planting styles of High Victorian patterned gardening. He is also credited with introducing the herbaceous border.

Although less well known than his contemporary Gertrude Jeykll his long-term influence on gardening is widely recognised. In 1933 when Robinson reached his 95th birthday, *The London Evening Standard* celebrated him as having 'changed the face of England'. His popular and persuasive writing style inspired generations and his later work *The English Flower Garden* (1883) was regarded as a 'bible' by many gardeners.

Above William Robinson and rhododendrons (From *The English Flower Garden*)

'Saint William'

Frederick formed a strong friendship with William Robinson and held him in such high esteem that he regarded him as a 'patron saint'. Although no documentary proof exists of Robinson ever visiting Emmetts, it is evident that he must have been familiar with it through correspondence. His influence can be clearly seen in the informal planting style which remains today such a distinctive characteristic.

'How these early frosts accentuate the essential difference between one style of garden and another ... bedded out plants, all 'dead men' and, in a few hours ... a pappy mass of corruption. Look now at the slimy putridity of plants which cannot compare in beauty or perfume with Rose, Carnation ...'

William Robinson, *The English Flower Garden*, 1883

A plantsman's paradise

The South Garden embodies a truly distinctive style of planting. Like a botanical stamp collection the trees and shrubs were carefully sited to grow to their own unique natural form, rather than placed in groups as part of a garden design. Most of the trees and shrubs here came from Veitch's nursery based at Coombe Wood in Surrey. All but two of these nursery specimens originated from China, a peculiarity that earns Emmetts a place amongst some of the greatest plant collections in south-east England. It is probable that many of these plants were bought when the nursery closed in 1914.

Above The South Garden

Right Rhododendron 'pink pearl'

The nurseries of James Veitch

Plant nurseries for the trading of exotic plants, trees and ferns rose to great prominence in the nineteenth century when gardening and horticulture grew in popularity amongst the middle-classes.

The Veitch Nurseries began as a small nursery near Exeter around 1808 under the charge of a young Scottish gardener named John Veitch. His expert gardening and landscaping work took him all over the country.

In 1837 he handed over the business to his son James, a man with a keen eye for business and quick to spot the money that could be made from selling exotic plants gleaned from foreign lands to the wealthy. James Veitch was one of the first commercial nurseries to sponsor their own plant collectors to explore foreign shores and seek out new and exciting plants for British gardens. By the mid-nineteenth century increased demand led to a second branch of the firm establishing itself in Chelsea. The business was passed down through the family, eventually coming under the control of Harry James Veitch at the turn of the century.

Over the course of 72 years the firm had employed the services of 23 plant collectors, to bring back plants and seeds from countries far and wide. By the outbreak of the First World War, the firm had been responsible for introducing an astonishing 1,281 plant species which were either previously unknown or newly bred varieties.

The age of plant collecting

English botanists and nurserymen had been prospecting the world for new plants since the end of the sixteenth century. The nineteenth century saw a great surge in interest for plant collecting as the demand for new and exotic plants increased amongst a new generation of wealthy garden owners.

The intrepid discoverers

Victorian plant hunters took to all corners of the world to find exotic plants to bring home, often risking their lives in the process. These plants were brought back for botanical collections and private gardens. Amongst the most well-known collectors is William Lobb (1809–64) who was responsible for the commercial introduction to England of the monkey-puzzle tree (*Araucaria araucana*) from Chile and the wellingtonia (*Sequoiadendron giganteum*) from North America.

The Wardian case

Up until the 1830s plants and seeds were transported in tubs, boxes and other containers which were prone to breakage and exposure to the elements. The Wardian case invented by Dr Nathaniel Bagshaw Ward (1791–1868) became the popular mode of transport from the mid-nineteenth century. The glazed case allowed tender plants to be set on deck to benefit from the sunlight and kept them protected from salt spray.

Lost in transit

Successfully seeking out plants and seeds in remote and difficult terrain may have been difficult enough, but for many expeditions this was just the start of their problems. Getting the plants and seeds safely back home was a hazardous affair. Exotic plants often succumbed to the ravages of long sea voyages and frequent changes in weather and temperature. Collector Peter Veitch lost a whole collection from Fiji when the ship transporting them ran aground in a gale.

Far left *Hortus Veitchi*, a study of the Veitch Nurseries, published in 1906

Left Peter Veitch

Opposite Hydrangea and *Eucryphia* in August

The quest for the dove tree

A Stunning Collection

The diverse collection of exotic trees and shrubs set amongst a backdrop of wildlife-rich woodland and meadows makes Emmetts a botanist's dream at any time of the year. A spectacular show of spring colours, the vibrant hues of summer and an autumnal display beyond compare, are a true feast for the senses. Such an abundance of pollen and nectar attracts a wealth of insect life in spring and summer months and the garden's bumblebees, hoverflies, butterflies and moths are our natural 'barometers' of a healthy garden.

Our Wild-flower Meadow has been allowed to develop naturally and the plants here such as yarrow, common knapweed, bird's-foot trefoil and sorrel are typical of the traditional hay meadows that would have bedecked many of the banks and hills of the area in times past. We allow the plants to flower and seed before cutting in late summer. The long grass is a perfect home for insects which in turn provide a valuable food source for birds and small mammals such as voles and shrews. Other mammals on the estate include dormice, which feed on nectar, berries and nuts from plants such as honeysuckle and hazel.

Bluebells and wild garlic in spring

Spring

Tree heather
Erica arborea

Camellia japonica

Winter hazel
Corylopsis pauciflora

Dove tree
Davidia involucrata

Chilean lantern tree
Crinodendron hookeranium

Barberry
Berberis darwinii

Star magnolia
Magnolia stellata

Magnolia 'Star Wars'

Common beech
Fagus sylvatica

Anenome blanda

Rhododendron 'Doncaster'

Wild tulip
Tulipa sylvestris

Rhododendron
'Prince Camille de Rohan'

Rhododendron luteum

Snowdrop tree
Halesia monticola

Rhododendron cinnabarinum

The dove or handkerchief tree is one of the garden's most enduring and treasured specimens. Its history here owes much to the intrepid feats of Ernest Wilson (1876–1930), a plant collector employed by Harry James Veitch.

'China Wilson'

In 1899 Harry James Veitch recruited Ernest Wilson to travel to China to seek out plants suitable for British gardens. Above all he was charged with bringing back the seed of the dove tree (*Davidia involucrata*). Wilson had been interested in plants from an early age, having worked as an apprentice gardener at the age of 16 at the Birmingham Botanical gardens. Naturally he was eager to take on the task.

Armed with a small sketch map of Sichuan Province marking the spot where the French missionary and collector Father Armand David, 'Pere' David (1826–1900), had found the dove tree in 1869, Wilson set off on his quest. He located the site of the tree but was dismayed to find that a local farmer had cut it down to use as timber in the building of a house. Undaunted, he was eventually able to find other specimens of the tree in the area. Despite having his boat wrecked on the rapids Wilson was able to save his specimens and they were brought back safely to Veitch's nursery on his return to England in 1902. On this one expedition alone Wilson collected over 300 seeds, tubers and corms, all gleaned from some of the most isolated and remote mountain valleys of the region. In time Frederick Lubbock was to purchase 35 different specimens of plants imported from this single expedition.

A horticultural hero

A man of legendary endurance, Wilson went on to complete many other expeditions, one of which was to leave him with a permanent injury: his leg was crushed by an avalanche of boulders as he was carried along the trail in his sedan chair. After setting his own leg with the tripod of his camera, he was carried back to civilization on a three-day forced march. Wilson's numerous expeditions to the Far East earned him the name 'China Wilson'.

A tale of love

According to local legend the dove tree is said to be the most romantic tree in China, an association which dates back to the Han dynasty. Zhaojun Wang married the king of a distant land and from 1,000 miles away sent a letter home by dove. The dove completed this journey landing on a tree covered in white doves outside her family's home where it died of exhaustion.

Autumn

Japanese maple
Acer palmatum

Fly agaric
Amanita muscaria

Dogwood
Cornus kousa

Full moon maple
Acer japonicum

Tulip tree
Liriodendron tulipifera

Paperbark maple
Acer griseum

Chinese tupelo
Nyssa sinensis

Leatherwood
Eucryphia 'Nymansay'

Atlantic cedar
Cedrus atlantica 'glauca'

English oak
Quercus robur

Dove tree
Davidia involucrata

Deciduous camellia
Stewartia pseudocamellia

Sorrel tree
Oxydendrum arboretum

Spindle tree
Euonymus europaeus

Mophead hydrangea
Hydrangea macrophylla

Winged spindle
Euonymus alatus

Summer

St John's wort
Hypericum 'Rowallane'

Brush bush
Eucryphia glutinosa

Magnolia watsonia

Masterwort
Astrantia major

Edelweiss
Leontopodium alpinum

Mexican fleabane
Erigeron karvinskianus

Field scabious
Knautia arvensis

Coneflower
Rudbeckia fulgida 'Goldsturm'

Montbretia *Crocosmia* 'Lucifer'

Opium poppy
Papaver somniferum

Rhododendron 'Polar Bear'

Opium poppy
Papaver somniferum 'Danish flag'

Floribunda rose
Rosa 'Escapade'

Monkey puzzle tree
Auracaria auracana

Cheddar pink
Dianthus gratianopolitanus

Climbing hydrangea
Hydrangea petiolaris

The Boise Years (1928–64)

Lubbock's death in 1927 heralded the beginning of a new chapter in the garden's history. An advertisement for the sale of the estate caught the eye of wealthy American geologist, Charles Watson Boise (1884–1964). In 1928 Charles and his wife Hazel moved into Emmetts and began to plant their own unique imprint on the gardens.

By the time Charles Boise moved into Emmetts he had made a successful career in the mineral prospecting industry. Born in North Dakota he began working in mining in Africa and in 1920 was responsible for making the first examination of diamond mining areas on the Gold Coast. His interest in diamonds continued and much of his later career was spent as an appraiser of these gems. In the late 1920s Charles was granted citizenship in the United Kingdom.

Phobias, fairways and fountains

Charles's geological expeditions in the tropics had left him with a fear of malaria and areas of standing water in which mosquitoes could breed. Such was his aversion that he decided to 'fill in' the ponds that Lubbock had created. Aside from this Charles respected the character and layout of the gardens that he had inherited. Most importantly he maintained the services of Lubbock's head gardener, George Taylor, who continued under Charles's employment for another 34 years.

Above Rock Garden gentians, c.1910

Left Charles Boise

Opposite The lily pond in the Rock Garden in August

Opposite top The Rose Garden

His changes were often therefore additions and alterations rather than radical makeovers. He had a strong interest in the Rock Garden and in 1937 began to develop this area to suit his own personal tastes. Under the supervision of a Miss Tyghe of Tunbridge Wells he brought in large blocks of Westmorland limestone to add more structure to this part of the garden.

His other lasting legacies include the addition of a copy of Andrea del Verrocchio's (1435–88) *Putto and Dolphin*, originally commissioned for the Medici family in Florence, as companion piece for the fountain in the Rose Garden. He also developed the herbaceous borders between the Rock Garden and the formal garden and created a six-hole golf course in the eastern area. In 1954 he started a propagation programme from Lubbock's plantings to ensure the botanical continuity of the garden.

His wife Hazel also had an interest in the garden and spent much time with wild flowers and roses 'to put the record straight' as she liked to say. She brought in small bright azaleas to the Alpine Garden.

Charles is fondly remembered as being very much part of village life and was happy to share his house and garden. He would invite the local children to Christmas dinner every year.

A Head Gardener's Tale

Ever since the Victorian era the success of any self-respecting garden of the wealthy depended upon the expertise of the head gardener. Often dedicating their whole lives to a single garden and revered for their horticultural expertise and commitment they are the forgotten heroes behind some of the country's most lavish gardens.

Head gardeners would typically begin an apprenticeship at an early age. They often commanded a large staff and were responsible for overseeing the planting and maintenance of all aspects of garden life. Some such as 'Capability Brown', gained national prestige and recognition and were sought out by wealthy landowners to create spectacular gardens. Most however quietly toiled away, steadfast and dedicated to their own cherished properties and places of work.

Crucially, in gardens like Emmetts, it was often the head gardeners that provided the much-needed continuity when owners passed on and estates changed hands. This characteristic loyalty is very much in evidence at Emmetts where in 100 years of the garden's history, from 1906 to 2006, just three head gardeners have occupied this privileged post.

George Taylor (1906–54)

George Taylor was the head gardener throughout most of Frederick Lubbock's period at Emmetts and then continued under Charles Boise when the property changed hands in 1928. Little is known of Mr Taylor or

'[He] was a marvellous gardener and a fine person. He liked children and would let me tag along in the garden and ask questions. He would also invite us to the lodge so we could see his tortoise and male cardinal bird.'

Taken from a letter from Anne Boise Beeler, the daughter of Charles and Hazel Boise

'Taylor' as he was known to his employers, but it is clear that he had a great passion for Emmetts and was a very strong driving force in the development of the garden and its design. Under Lubbock, he was responsible for a team of up to 14 gardeners.

George Joy (1954–82)

From 1954 to 1982 George Joy was employed as head gardener first under Charles Boise and then later under the National Trust. He was a student at Cambridge University Botanic Garden from 1936 to 1938 and then at Kew until 1940. During the Second World War he served in Iceland with the Worcester Regiment, and then joined the Royal Artillery. After the War he returned briefly to Kew and other nurseries before moving to Emmetts.

He further developed the plant collection begun by the Lubbock and Boise families and was particularly responsible for the development of the Rock Garden. He was by all accounts a strong-minded man and had a team of four gardeners working under him. Memories of these times recall that one of

Above George Fillis in the Rock Garden

Right Rhododendrons in the North Garden (*please note the House is closed to the public*)

Below Storm damage, 1987

these gardeners was a heavy smoker, whilst another adopted an entertaining means of sending messages to his wife whilst he was at work. By climbing one of the garden trees and waving two tea cloths he was able to convey his amorous after-work intentions by semaphore!

George Fillis (1982–2006)

George Fillis, son of a woodsman from Canterbury, came to occupy the post in 1982. George had four or five assistant gardeners working for him. Under his charge he saw the complete restoration of the North Garden. One of the greatest challenges came with the aftermath of the 'great storm' of October 1987, in which around 95 per cent of the trees at Emmetts were blown down including many of the trees and shrubs planted by Lubbock. The storm did, however, provide a once in a lifetime opportunity to look at the gardens afresh. George and his garden staff undertook an extensive and sympathetic replanting programme that has now restored Emmetts to being one of the most popular and visited gardens in Kent.

Mark Nelson (2006–11)

The arrival of Mark Nelson as head gardener in 2006 broke the longstanding association of 'Georges' with the gardens. Mark's passion for the garden and its history inspired projects such as the Rock Garden restoration and the repair of the ram pump (see p.29). The stewardship of the garden has now passed to a new head gardener, Simon Walker, who with his team of expanding volunteers aims to continue its restoration.

A Children's Garden

Frederick Lubbock's arrival at Emmetts heralded not only a transformation and expansion of the gardens as a horticultural masterpiece but also the creation of a new and treasured space for his family and their outdoor pursuits. Just as now, the English garden was a life-shaping backdrop for play, adventure and education.

Both Frederick and Catherine had come from large families and their childhood experiences, at play in idyllic surroundings, naturally set a fitting template upon which they modelled their own children's early years. Later the house and gardens would become the perfect setting for the next generation, with

Catherine and Frederick as grandparents presiding over a huge family of grandsons and daughters, nephews and nieces.

An outside classroom

Gardens were just as important for scholarly pursuits, none more so than the simple enjoyment of reading and listening. The tradition is well evidenced from Percy Lubbock's fond recollections of childhood visits to the Gurney home at Earlham where on a hot afternoon 'before long the children were being read to while they were held to their repose on the brown rug'. The tradition was certainly very much part of childhood at Emmetts through the generations. Catherine Lubbock would apparently use the garden as a place to read aloud to her

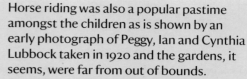

Horse riding was also a popular pastime amongst the children as is shown by an early photograph of Peggy, Ian and Cynthia Lubbock taken in 1920 and the gardens, it seems, were far from out of bounds.

Opposite left **Peggy Lubbock and Grandfather, 1914**

Opposite below **Peggy and Michael Lubbock with a wigwam, 1915.**

Left **The Wild-flower Meadow**

Below **Cartwheeling in the Wild-flower Meadow**

grandchildren in the 1920s: 'Among their happiest memories were her reading aloud of Dickens, on the white seat under the may tree on the lawn at Emmetts'.

We can imagine that similar memories of the Churchill children at nearby Chartwell would have struck a chord with the Lubbock household where literature in the garden became a kind of sport: 'Great lashings of poetry were stashed away inside us and on the long summer evenings, when we would be sleeping out in the garden, it became fun to see how long we could keep reciting poetry and even bits of famous prose'.

The tradition lives on

Today the gardens at Emmetts continue to provide a cherished area for family relaxation and recreation. The Wild-flower Meadow provides an ideal spot to relax, play and enjoy the views, while a variety of trails and activities for families are available to help explore the gardens.

Tour of the Garden

The northern areas comprising the 'themed gardens' for roses, smaller shrubs, herbaceous plants, alpines, and dwarf rhododendrons are cherished examples of Edwardian ornamental gardening at its most spectacular. Rich in growth and ever-changing throughout the seasons it was these areas that provided the 'bread and butter' work for the busy team of gardeners.

The Rose Garden

Created for Catherine Lubbock between 1910 and 1920, the Rose Garden was very much a central feature of the original garden design. It formed a frame for one of the key vistas from the house out towards the valley and Weald of Kent.

In the Lubbocks' time a smaller square pond formed the centrepiece. Early photos show that it held a far more diverse range of herbaceous plants than today with standard roses, swags of roses on the terrace between the garden and the house, and large planters on the path.

Above The Rose Garden today

Left The Rose Garden, c.1910

The Alpine and Rock Garden

'… most alpine plants can be grown in the open ground, with little hillocks and ridges thrown up, so as to provide different aspects, and dryer or moister positions, than in the more imposing 'artificial' rockery constructions … '

An extract from William Robinson's *Alpine Flowers for English Gardens*, 1893

Above The Rock Garden looking towards Ide Hill, *c.*1910

Right The Rock Garden today

The Rock Garden was laid out by Frederick Lubbock around the same time as the Rose Garden, and was to provide a haven for his alpine plant collection. Originally this part of the garden extended around the outside of the Rose Garden hedge, giving a greater area than the modern-day layout.

The building of special garden features to imitate mountainsides, streams and rocky outcrops dates from the late eighteenth century but it was the Victorian gardener and author William Robinson who first championed the idea of using alpine plants to fill them. Until then the fashion had been for over-engineered formal rockeries, a practice that both Robinson and Lubbock disliked.

By the time Charles Boise took on the house and gardens in 1928 the Alpine Garden must have been a well-established feature with perhaps more than 40 different species of plants. Mrs Boise Beeler (see p.20) describes it when her parents arrived as composed of 'heathery banks and a winding path'. It is probable that Charles Boise installed the pond at the same time as introducing the Westmorland Limestone in the late 1930s.

'There are many disappointments in growing alpines, as with everything else, but they afford a constant and daily interest, and given a breezy open situation and a deep light soil, there should be many more successes than failures.'

Frederick Lubbock quoted in: *Alpine Flowers for English Gardens* by William Robinson, 1893

The South Garden

The South Garden is home to an impressive collection of hardy exotic trees and shrubs and was laid out by Frederick Lubbock around the turn of the twentieth century in two phases; the first half between 1896 and 1909 and the second half after 1909 up to the First World War. The present-day collection is largely still that of Frederick Lubbock, many gleaned from plant collector Ernest Wilson's Chinese expeditions on behalf of Veitch's Nursery.

The South Garden Planting Plan

1 Japanese umbrella pine *(Sciadopitys verticillata)*
   Its needle-like leaves resemble the ribs of an umbrella. Originates from the Triassic period – the age before dinosaurs.
   Origin: Japan
2 Brewer's weeping spruce *(Picea breweriana)*
   An evergreen tree with drooping swathes of dark green foliage.
   Origin: two small areas of the Siskiyou Mountains on the Oregon/Californian border, USA
3 The dove or handkerchief tree *(Davidia involucrata)*
   Introduced to western cultivation by Ernest Wilson, 1899 (see p.14).
   Origin: China
4 Prickly castor-oil tree *(Kalopanax septemlobus)*
   Spiky-stemmed tree with large flower heads.
   Origin: China and Japan
5 Japanese maple *(Acer palmatum)*
   A large maple with beautiful foliage.
   Origin: Japan, East Asia
6 Paper-bark maple *(Acer griseum)*
   A small tree with eye-catching bark. Introduced to western cultivation by Ernest Wilson, 1901
   Origin: China

7 Winged spindle *(Euonymus alatus)*
   Produces bright red foliage in winter and autumn.
   Origin: Japan and central China
8 Burnt toffee tree *(Katsura cercidiphyllum japonicum)*
   The autumn foliage smells of burnt brown sugar, or candyfloss. Ernest Wilson introduced it to western civilisation after he brought back seeds from his 3rd Expedition to China 1907–1909.
   Origin: Japan and China
9 Scots pine *(Pinus sylvestris)*
   A large evergreen tree – see the five trees planted in a row.
   Origin: Europe and Asia
10 Persian Silk Tree *(Albizia julibrissin)*
   Produces masses of fragrant pink, pom-pom like flowers in summer. In 1918 Ernest Wilson collected its seeds in South Korea.
   Origin: East Asia
11 Tree Cotoneaster *(Cotoneaster frigidus)*
   A shrub producing vivid berries red in autumn.
   Origin: China and the Himalayas
12 Prickly heath *(Gaultheria mucronata)*
   A small evergreen shrub with vibrant purple/pink berries in autumn.
   Origin: Chile
13 Snake-bark maple *(Acer capillipes)*
   Named because of its stripy bark, it was introduced to western cultivation by Ernest Wilson in 1901.
   Origin: China.
14 Blue Atlas cedar *(Cedrus atlantica* 'Glauca')
   One of the largest trees in the garden with striking blue-green foliage.
   Origin: Atlas Mountains in Algeria and Morocco.

14

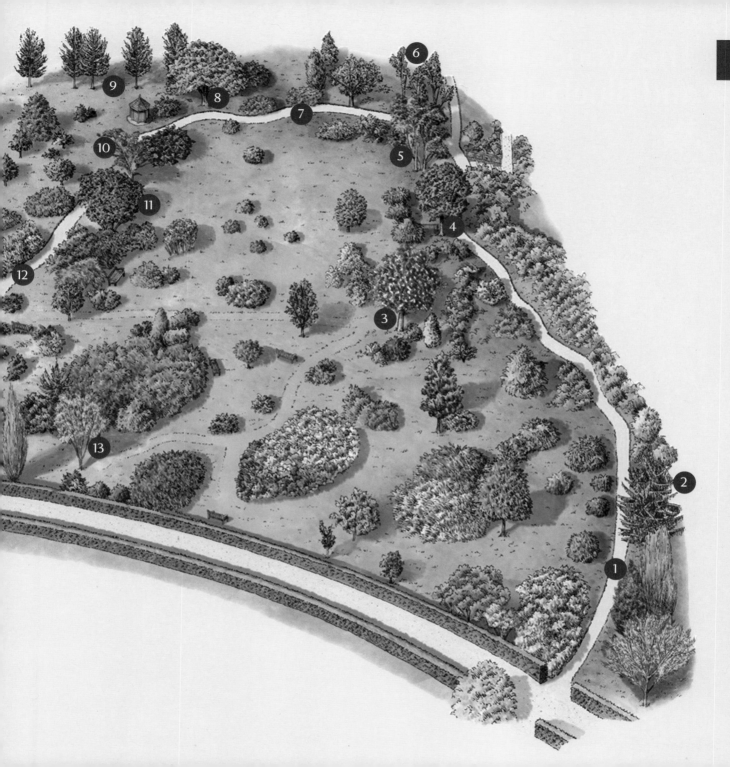

The Woodland and Bluebell Bank

Left Pink camellias in spring

Right An orange tip butterfly on a bluebell

The Bluebell Bank represents one of Lubbock's final phases of garden expansion, providing an attractive transition from the formality of the conventional gardens to the untamed natural order of the surrounding countryside and woodland. It also affords spectacular views across the Weald of Kent. The area suffered much damage in the 1987 storm.

The 'wild hyacinth'

Widely distributed and common throughout the United Kingdom, bluebells have long been cherished as one of the nation's favourite flowers. They thrive in shady habitats such as broadleaved woodland where they can dominate the ground flora, though they also occur in hedgerows, alongside bracken and in open grassland, particularly in the damper western parts of Britain.

The flower has been variously known as 'wild hyacinth' and 'crow's toes'. 'Bluebell' came into popular use after the romantic poets began to celebrate the plant in the early nineteenth century.

Bluebell lore

Bluebells are famous for their folklore. In times past, when forests were forbidding places, people believed that the bells rang out to summon fairies to their gatherings. Alas, any human who heard a bluebell ring would soon die. A field of bluebells was thought to be associated with fairy enchantments.

The Ram Pump

Directly below the bluebell bank lie a pond and the original Ram Pump that used to supply Emmetts House and gardens with water. It was installed in 1906 and was manufactured by a local foundry and has recently been restored. It is now once again pumping water back into the garden.

The ram or hydraulic pump was pioneered by Joseph Montgolfier, the French inventor of the hot-air balloon. He succeeded in making a self-acting pump in 1796 which works on the principle of using a large amount of water falling through a small height to lift a smaller amount of the same water to a much greater height.

See the pump in action by following the footpath from the Tea Room down into the woods.

Explore the Estate

Emmetts Garden is one of a group of National Trust properties centred around the much-loved area of Toys Hill. Straddling the greensand ridge of hills the National Trust estate encompasses more than 180 hectares of woodland, much of which is managed for its wildlife interest.

Right Pastel drawing of *Octavia Hill*, by Samuel Laurence

Opposite The view to Ide Hill

A natural treasure

Most of the estate woodland is recognised for its nature conservation interest and is designated as the Scords Wood and Brockhoult Mount Site of Special Scientific Interest (SSSI). A number of plants which are uncommon in Kent occur in the site, including southern wood-rush, spiked wood-sedge, lily-of-the-valley, common wintergreen, lemon-scented fern and the nationally scarce narrow-leaved helleborine. The woodland also supports a number of notable mosses and liverworts.

The National Trust maintains the woodland habitats through management such as cutting (coppicing). In some areas clearance is undertaken to restore heathland plants such as heather and bilberry, characteristic of the area in times past when the 'common' was much more open.

A network of well-maintained paths and tracks provides the perfect way of exploring these beautiful woodlands and a range of guided routes and circuits makes Emmetts the perfect place to start a walk. Within easy reach lie the Octavia Hill woodlands, Weardale Manor ruins, and Toys Hill viewpoints. Alternatively, follow the Weardale walk from Emmetts to visit nearby Chartwell, family home of Sir Winston Churchill. Pick up the trail leaflets at the visitor information point.

Fungi heaven

The damp woodlands provide ideal conditions for fungi. Look out for the distinctive red and white spotted fly agaric or the smelly stinkhorn, but don't touch as many fungi are poisonous.

Octavia Hill Woodlands

Octavia Hill (1821–96) was one of the founders of the National Trust and lived nearby at Crockham Hill. She is buried in the churchyard of Holy Trinity Church, Crockham Hill. Visit the terrace with a sunken well that she donated to the National Trust in 1898.

A home with a view

Situated close to one of the highest points in Kent, Emmetts has long been renowned for its breathtaking views across the Weald of Kent. The 'Grand Panoramic views of the surrounding country' as detailed in the sale particulars for the house in 1890 remain an enduring attraction today. To the south a patchwork of woodlands and meadows dotted with villages and hamlets stretches deep into the neighbouring county of East Sussex, while to the east and north the view is framed by the high ridge of the North Downs.

What next for Emmetts?

Conservation and restoration of the garden has been at the heart of the National Trust's work ever since it was bequeathed the land in 1964. Much of this has focused on maintaining and restoring the original character and planting schemes laid out by its previous owners. Sadly the 'great storm' of October 1987 destroyed large swathes of the garden and many of the mature specimen trees were lost. Thanks to the dedicated work of the National Trust gardening staff and volunteers much of the garden has recovered from this devastation.

Above The Tulip Garden, c.1910

Below The Tulip Garden under restoration

The remarkable discovery in 2009 of four sets of stereoscopic glass slides dating to around 1910 belonging to John Pym, Frederick Lubbock's great grandson, has added a new and exciting dimension to the restoration work. The slides give a fascinating insight into the layout of the gardens in Lubbock's time and provide the much-needed detail that has enabled an ambitious restoration project to unfold.

A five-year conservation plan began in 2009 with the restoration of the Rock Garden, a project which has involved bringing in 95 tonnes of Kentish ragstone to re-create the Scree Garden of the early 1900s. Slides of the Rose Garden have similarly allowed reconstruction of the rose swag walk. More recently attention has focused on the restoration of the pond in the South Garden. Future plans include restoring the Pinetum and highlighting and accentuating the summer features and planting that lie hidden within the garden.

The new garden 'staff'

Whereas previous head gardeners commanded a team of paid gardeners and apprentices, changing times mean that properties such as Emmetts rely increasingly on the vibrant and enthusiastic body of National Trust volunteers to help maintain the gardens. We are always keen to recruit new volunteers so if you are interested please speak to a member of staff.